IMAGES OF ENGLAND

BURNLEY
REVISITED

IMAGES OF ENGLAND

BURNLEY
REVISITED

MICHAEL TOWNEND

TEMPUS

*Again for Sam and Sophie whose history is still, though a little bit less,
in the future.*

Frontispiece: Photographers will do anything for a snap: Rock Water,
Cliviger, 1888.

First published 2006

Tempus Publishing Limited
The Mill, Brimscombe Port,
Stroud, Gloucestershire, GL5 2QG
www.tempus-publishing.com

British Library Cataloguing in Publication Data.
A catalogue record for this book is available from the British Library.

ISBN 0 7524 3996 0

Typesetting and origination by Tempus Publishing Limited.
Printed in Great Britain.

Contents

Acknowledgements

I would like to thank the following: Dave Anderson, Eric Anderson, Joan Barber, David Barrowclough, Harry Bartram, Philip Bennett, Bert Blackburn, Ken Bolton Collection, Susan Bourne, Alan Bradfield, Briercliffe Society, Florence Brown, Burnley Borough Council, *Burnley Express*, Ann Clark, John Coates, Noel Coates, Roger Frost, Brian Hall, Bob Hanna, Ken Hare, Alice Harris, Alan Harrison, Robert Hayhurst, Eric Hebdon, James Howell, Dianna Hudson, John Hutchinson, Margaret Hutchinson, Stuart James, Derek Jenkins, Margaret Jones, Dr Tony Kitto, Lancashire County Library and Information Service: Burnley Library, *Lancashire Evening Telegraph*, Lowerhouse Cricket Club, Alan Mackay, Marks & Spencer PLC, Marjorie Moore, Richard Harvey Morgan, Harry and Rosalie Newsham, Virginia O'Connor, Daniel O'Connor, Oddie's Bakery, Neil Riley, Allen Rycroft, Colin and Cynthia Sanderson, Janice Scott, Peter Sewell, Walter Sharp, Edith Sheldrick, Harry Simpson, Kirstie Simpson, Irene Slater, Nick Smith, Jean Smith, Dot Soltau, Janis Southworth, Doreen Sunter, David Sutcliffe, Mike Taylor, Kathleen Taylor, Joyce Taylor, Angela Timms, Patrick Wearden, Dennis White, Ray Wilcock and finally Ken Spencer, without whose knowledge and enthusiasm Burnley would be much the poorer.

Introduction

Images of England: Burnley was published in 1999. All the photographs for that volume came from the collections in Towneley Hall, Burnley's art gallery and museum since 1903. When choosing photographs for this book the collections in Towneley did not have enough variety or quality. So, about half of the images here have been borrowed from other people and collections. This gave access to photographs, many of which have never been seen before let alone published.

In many cases, the selection was easy. In others it was not. The postcard of St John's, Cliviger (p.109) would not normally have been included because it is a very common print – it was the message on the reverse which was puzzling and interesting. It also shows something of the standard of literacy at the time.

Improved technology has meant more detail can be seen in the photographs. A close study of an ambrotype – a Victorian photograph on glass – of a man with a cart (p.65), shows he is a fish seller but only a few letters in his name can be identified. Additional historical sources suggest his name was Hitchon.

Other photographs were chosen not because of the view (or messages on postcards) but because of how they could be used to highlight the social history of the town. Many examples are here. With others, personal reminiscences are used. When John Hutchinson spoke to me about the tragic day at Hapton Valley Colliery, he was *there*. Similarly, the group of wedding photographs relies heavily on the memories of children and in one case the couple themselves. With some, memories are more than reflective. Richard Harvey Morgan (p.113) was asked to write his own memories when he was ten years old. The script is one of a child's – quickly moving from one subject to another – but he wrote about what stuck in his mind.

Who were these photographers? There is a mixture of professional, skilled amateurs and happy snappers. George Henry Foulds (overleaf) was photographed, aged about twenty-three, by Sam Lancaster. Sam had several jobs, including photography, with premises on Curzon Street. George himself acquired these in the 1890s and went on to run a successful business in Burnley and Simonstone. Later he practiced as a dentist.

Richard Broughton specialised in postcards. He worked in a cotton mill before going into business. His studio was on Woodbine Road. Because his income was dependent on sales he produced a large number of different photographs of the same event and place. Those cards featuring people were almost guaranteed successful sales: 'Can you see me on this card?' and 'If you hold this to the light I am the one with the pinhole through the chest' were typical phrases written on the back of many postcards. Richard also photographed in Rossendale, Cumbria and Yorkshire.

Other photographers were amateurs. Daniel Drew was featured in the first volume and a few of his other photographs are here. Daniel could afford several expensive cameras and his hobby was virtually confined to the family, the factory he ran and his interest in sailing. On the other hand, Bert Sturgeon took photographs using much cheaper cameras. But these 'snaps' are no less important. Again the emphasis was on work and family but it is clear he thought specifically about their composition.

Others include Tommy Robinson who only seems to have taken photographs of the Lowerhouse, Rosegrove and Accrington Road areas. This was a sideline to his normal work as a painter and decorator. Milford Wright has one photograph in the book. Perhaps his story is the strangest of all. What made the American-born Milford travel from his birthplace to South Africa, Europe, Scotland and finally Burnley is unknown. On the way he developed his stereoscopic photography business. In Burnley, his studio was on Hollingreave Road. He used his family, himself and neighbours as 'models' on many occasions. However, relatively few of his photographs of Burnley have been found.

Michael Townend
Towneley Hall, Burnley, 2006

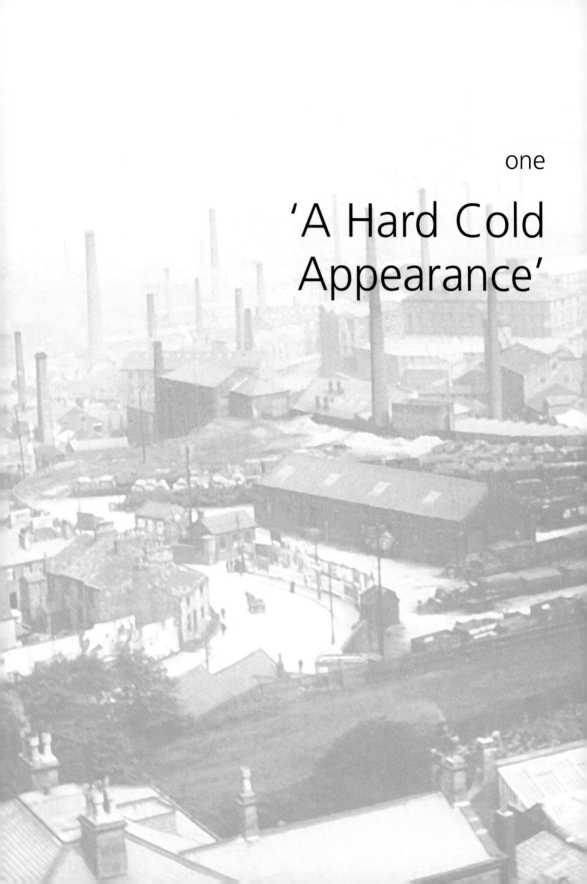

one

'A Hard Cold Appearance'

Burnley, *c.* 1905. The town centre's layout was complete when this photograph was taken from Manchester Road Chapel. The railway at Manchester Road and to Colne effectively marked the town centre boundary. Behind the photographer were larger houses, and west of the railway to Colne was the extensive view to Pendle Hill. The town is virtually free of smoke. This suggests the photograph was taken in Burnley Fair week when the air would be clearer.

Opposite above: Manchester Road, *c.* 1890. Partly called 'South Parade' this was one of the 'gates' out of town. The site of the first Manchester Road railway station was here. The photographer called this picture 'Manchester Road from Catch Penny Hill'. It is thought this is the only time Springhill has been referred to by this name.

Opposite below: Trafalgar Street, *c.* 1910. The street runs in front of Thorneybank Mill (the building with the tall arched windows). On the left is the textile iron works of Butterworth and Dickinson ('Butts & Dicks'). Behind the left-hand chimney is the Weavers' Institute in the Meadows district, an area of densely built housing.

P.S.205-4.

ON THE WAY TO STEPPING STONES
PARK LANE BURNLEY.

Park Lane, *c.* 1906. Countryside was, and still is, never far away. The walk to the stepping stones was very popular, especially during bank holidays. The message on the postcard reads: '... a view of the local countryside here. Note the limestone road, very bad for the eyes when the sun is shining. For particulars see small bills'.

Opposite above: Godly Bridge, 1888. The track beyond was the Thursby family's private road along the Ridge connecting Bank Hall and Ormerod House. Other people using the road had to pay a toll. From 1908, the toll proceeds were given to charity.

Opposite below: From the Ridge, 1935. The building (right centre) was known as the 'turning place'. This was where ginny tracks met and changed direction. A ginny was a small railway on which coal trucks ran guided by a chain. Ginnies from Beehole Colliery (near Turf Moor) and Rowley Colliery were directed from here to the canal near Albert Street and Bank Hall Colliery via Queen's Park.

Composite, looking south, 1961. Centenary Way is being laid out. To the left the Central Transport Garage has a distinctive roofline. The building was seen as a feat of engineering but part of it collapsed a few years later. Dominant are the electricity and cleansing 'destructor' works chimneys. To the left, Burnley Wood was one of the last main areas of population to be laid out in the 1880s. These tended to be better-quality terraced houses when compared with the older ones on Finsleygate. The oldest surviving buildings (in 2006) are Finsley Mill (1866) and Aenon Chapel (1851).

Opposite above: Moseley Road in the 1930s. The smallholdings in Towneley were popular in the 1930s. One person recalls: 'I was born in a semi-detached house. It had a living room, a parlour, three bedrooms, a bathroom, a pantry and a kitchen. It had electricity, it had gas but it didn't have sewerage'. Produce from the land was often sold as a sideline. For some it led to a new business: 'during the 1930s he had his own egg and fresh chicken round. He kept hundreds of poultry'.

Opposite below: From the Corporation's 'destructor' chimney, 1962. The town centre had, in close proximity, old housing, chapels, iron works, the cattle market, theatres, and the gas and electric works. Older buildings had a grimy appearance due to the smoke from factory and domestic chimneys. The police station and magistrates' court opened in 1955, occupying the site of the bus station on the cattle market. The first Clean Air Act and industrial decline meant a reduction in smoke pollution. As a result, new buildings remained new looking. In the 1960s, much of this area was swept away with the demolition of older buildings, including Brunswick Chapel opposite the Town Hall.

Barden tip, 4 October 1950. Prominent are the Oswald Street Gas Works opened in 1928 and John Grey's mills. Grey's was one of the larger cotton firms. Their Livingstone and Cameron Mills were, unusually for Burnley, brick built. PenDelfin (famous for their stoneware, especially rabbits) occupied Cameron Mill in 1973. The site of a brick works (see p.55) is in the foreground. Livingstone Mill was demolished in 2006.

M65 motorway, 1981. The three forms of transport, canal, railway and motorway, brought a change to the landscape as well as the economy. All follow similar routes into east Lancashire. The motorway brought residential, retail and industrial development to new areas and helped expand older ones.

two

Town Centre

Above: Church Street, *c.* 1886. The medieval heart of the town was here. Part of the market house was in the building in the centre. Behind is the Talbot. To the right are the remains of the second market cross and stocks, last used in the 1850s. This area, known as 'Top o' th' Town', was redeveloped and the street widened shortly after the photograph was taken. The name may have been the basis of a children's rhyme, with similar actions to 'Little Piggy'. The rhyme ended with the words 'little tippy top o' th' town ender'.

Above: St Peter's Church, *c.* 1884. Although the town centre had moved away from the church, it remained the most important building in town. The churchyard was the main burial ground until the cemetery opened. Family and social historians study inscriptions and gain much information from the gravestones. They range from the tragic: 'here lieth ye body of John Riley 1744 and 13 of his children', to sudden death.

Right: St Peter's Church, *c.* 1914. Gravestones outside and memorials inside the church are important to local historians. The three memorials above the door refer to the Hargreaves family, who owned a number of coal mines. On the left is Henry Blakeborough's, a clockmaker whose 1820s clock is on Towneley Hall. On the right, the memorial is to the Revd Miles Greenwood who died in China.

Opposite below: Shorey Well, *c.* 1890. The well was the main source of water for the old town centre, around St Peter's Church. The water was seen to have mystical qualities and was still in use in the drought of 1887. The structure was moved to the grounds of the grammar school in 1906.

St James' Street, 1881. By the mid-nineteenth century, the town centre had moved to the St James' Street and Manchester Road area. Shops on the street included: ironmongers, chemists, drapers, confectioners, watchmakers and auctioneers. The scene would soon change when tramway lines were laid, and again in the early 1900s when the street was widened.

St James' Street, c. 1899. Featured centrally is the 'gawmless' lamp. The first gas lamp was erected in 1823. An electric one replaced it seventy years later. Opposite is the 'Bull'. Stagecoaches ran from here and various functions took place in the building, from special celebrations to inquests.

St James' Street, *c.* 1882. The Mason's Arms and Bay Horse Hotel (left) were built in the early nineteenth century. In 1829, of the twenty-six inns, hotels and taverns, most were in the town centre. In 1834, as a reaction to the 'evils of drink', the Temperance movement came to Burnley. Two years later a medal was awarded to a Mr Whalley, 'King of the Reformed Drunkards'. Despite the movement having many followers, the number of pubs rose. In 1899, there were ninety-seven hotels, inns and taverns as well as ninety-three beerhouses in the town.

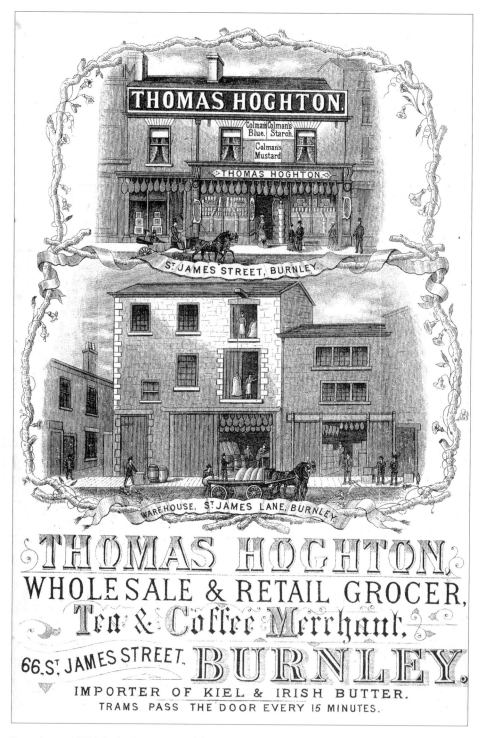

Paper bag, *c.* 1885. The business was established on St James' Street in around 1870 and was open about twenty years. In many cases, engravings such as these are the only images we have of buildings. The bag is in Towneley Hall's collection.

St James' Street, *c.* 1906. Victoria Theatre, on the right, opened in 1886 and was demolished shortly after closing in 1955. On the left, the three circular globes hanging above the street make a pawnbroker's sign. This was an essential shop for many people. Possessions were pawned for money and then redeemed at a later date. Opposite were two ice cream shops, a saddler and a watchmaker.

St James' Street, *c.* 1926. The Golden Padlock hardware store is on the right. Street furniture such as the padlock was important for advertising and informed people what the shop sold. A shop in Cliviger Street to the left was used as a film location in *A Kind of Loving*. The town was also shown in *The Man in the White Suit* and *Whistle Down the Wind*.

St James' Street, *c.* 1958. A composite photograph taken a few years before the town centre was redeveloped. Signs of this are here: the Keirby Hotel, which opened in 1960, is being built. Suspended above the street is a light which, when lit, indicated a police emergency. There was a police box further up the street. Bridge Street is running down left of centre. A sign on the pole on Bridge Street is urging people to 'Keep Britain Tidy', a campaign started in around 1955.

Opposite above: Marks & Spencer, 1935. The store was built on the site of the Royal Oak pub. The company was the third large retail firm (after Woolworths and Burton's) to come to Burnley. On opening, staff were asked, and agreed, to contribute 2d from their wages every week to the Victoria Hospital fund. Public subscription and support enabled the hospital to keep running. A modern-day parallel is Pendleside Hospice, which receives twenty-five per cent of its funding from the NHS, with the rest coming from fundraising and public support.

Opposite below: St James' Street, 1935. This was the last year the trams ran, as buses replaced them. The first Corporation bus ran in 1924 although private buses had been running since the early 1900s. Rishton Mill, whose tower is in the background, was demolished in 1936 to be replaced by the Odeon Cinema. Opposite the trams was the 'drag': a stretch of pavement where people paraded to show themselves off.

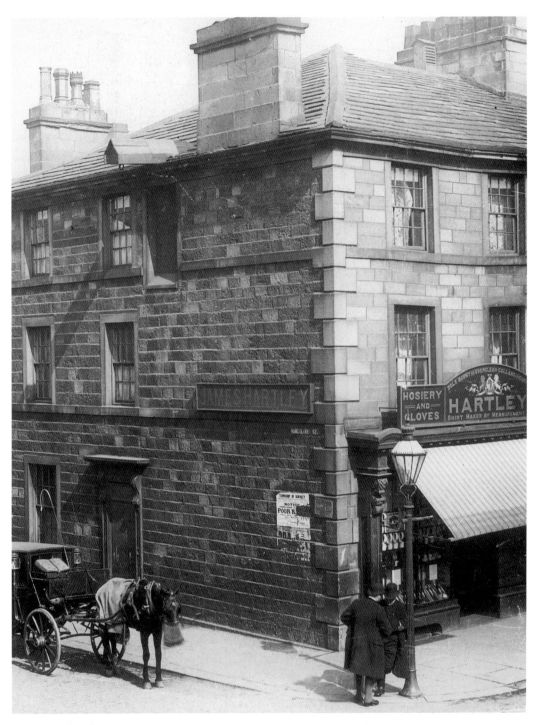

Manchester Road, *c.* 1882. Drapers used the shop before and after James Hartley's short occupation in the early 1880s. The poster is concerned with the poor rate and the town's relief of the poor that culminated in the opening of the main workhouse in 1877. Gas lighting (as well as water utilities) was introduced in the early nineteenth century. The last horse 'cabby' retired in 1930.

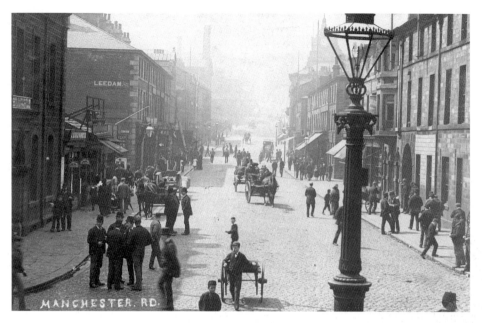

Manchester Road, *c.* 1890. Unusually, the photograph was taken at 11 a.m. from the top deck of a tram. Tramlines were laid in Manchester Road in 1903-04. They were extended to the 'summit' in 1910, thus giving service to the south and one of the more prosperous areas of town.

Manchester Road, *c.* 1890. The row of shops included Bell's, a silk draper, hat, fur, dress and milliners. There was also a boot maker, jeweller and tailor. The bollards were to stop traffic cutting across the pavement. Grimshaw Street (right) was the commercial centre of town.

Manchester Road, *c.* 1907. The shops between Hargreaves Street and Yorke Street included Cunningham's, an opticians/jewellers; Bright's, a stationer; and Johnson Brothers, dyers and dry cleaners. Heavy window blinds were a feature of many shops. Many of these were made in the town.

Yorkshire Street, 1926. The new aqueduct ('culvert') carrying the canal was built in 1926. To accommodate increasing vehicle traffic this replaced a late eighteenth-century structure. The wagon is from the Burnley Co-operative stores. The forty-seat tram was built in 1920 with an English electric body on a Burnley-built bogie.

Market Street, 1887. Shops on the street included tailors and clothiers, butchers, Lawson's tea dealers and John Gutteridge's stationers. Bill posting was used throughout the town for publicising news, events and auctions as well as advertising. Burnley's streets were some of the most heavily bill-posted in Lancashire.

Market Street, 1960s. Like many other pubs, the New Market Hotel was a conversion from a private house. The building was a venue for a music hall and boxing matches. More recently, the Garrick Theatre Club was based here. Other pubs had live theatre and one, the Barracks Tavern, had a museum.

Hammerton Street, *c.* 1910. The Co-operative central stores dominated the street. Their first purpose-built store was opened in 1862. Extensions and new buildings followed. In the centre is a former cotton mill, being used by Proctor's to make their world-famous mechanical boiler stokers.

Opposite: Market Hall, 1960s. The hall was opened in 1870 and signified not only a change in shopping habits but also civic pride. The pot fair poster suggests the photograph was taken at or near Burnley Fair in July. The last pot fair was held in 2003. The last remnant of Burnley Fair and the local holidays in east Lancashire – the school holiday pattern – was changed in 2006.

Aenon Baptist Chapel, *c.* 1852. A group from the Ebenezer Baptists founded the chapel in 1850. The first service in the (unfinished) Red Lion Street building was held in 1851. The chapel opened a year later. In 1891, the two main Baptist movements joined. The General Baptist Association met at Aenon and voted to join the Particular Baptists to form the Baptist Union. As well as religion, the Nonconformists played an important part in the moral and social life of the town. The final service at Aenon was held in 1989.

Opposite above: Bethel Chapel Choir, 1867. Bethel (Primitive Methodist) was one of thirty-nine Nonconformist chapels in Burnley. Founded in 1829, a new chapel was built on Hammerton Street in 1852. Rules in the early days included: 'we do not allow young men and young women to court with each other on Sunday … our singers, the girls, are not allowed to wear bows on their bonnets'. This is one of the earliest group photographs taken in Burnley.

Opposite below: Wesleyan Chapel, Hargreaves Street, 1908. Attendance in churches and chapels reached a peak at about this time. John Wesley visited the town several times in the 1780s. The first Wesleyan chapel was built at Keighley Green in 1788. This one was the second, built in 1840. The building could seat 1,600 people and its school was on Red Lion Street. Behind is the chimney of the Victoria dyeworks and on the right is St James' Row, laid out in 1834 and 1841. The chapel was demolished in 1965.

Red Lion Street, 1961. The Savoy Cinema on the left opened in 1922 as a picture house and café and it was the first to screen 'talkies'. The cinema had been closed for five years before its demolition to make way for a bank. The large chimney was the 'destructor' chimney. Here, people's refuse was burnt and sometimes pets were given 'a bobs worth'; that is, they were electrocuted.

three

Out and About

Queen's Park, c. 1900. The move to develop urban parks from the mid-Victorian period was the result of civic pride and was seen as a way of improving public health. The movement came late to Burnley. People already had access to the Bank Hall grounds as well as a number of recreation areas. Queen's was opened in 1893 due to the generosity of the Thursby family, who provided land for the park.

Towneley Hall, c. 1909. The canopy on the left was built shortly after the museum opened in 1903. Here, visitors could buy a museum guide and leave their parasols or sticks for 1d. In one year, £166 was raised. Of this, £55 was spent on the oil painting 'Blind Beggar'. This was the first oil painting bought by the museum.

Ivory collection, Towneley Hall. When the museum opened there was little to show the public. It was thought that seeing items from different cultures would educate people. So, collections came from overseas. William Taylor sent items from his travels overseas, Lady O'Hagan donated Egyptian objects, Herbert Wright sent objects from Sri Lanka, and George Eastwood bequeathed his collection of ivories.

Edward Stocks Massey Gallery, Towneley Hall, 1960s. The watercolour gallery was named after a local benefactor to the arts. The collection of watercolours was largely developed in the 1920s and '30s. The skylights were filled and air conditioning installed to improve the environmental conditions for the collections. The room was converted into a school room and natural history gallery in 2006.

Worsthorne Square. As with other areas of the town, the Thursby family influenced Worsthorne's development. The Revd William Thursby was incumbent at St John's Church and the family paid for the church as well as a new church tower and font in 1903. The family also paid for the assembly rooms to the right of the café, built in 1874.

Theiveley (sic) Farm, c. 1910. Thieveley Farm and Pike were popular destinations for day trippers, especially before the First World War. Many people caught the train to Holme and then walked to the farm, where refreshments could be bought and games, swing boats and donkey rides enjoyed. The attraction became less popular in the 1920s.

Haggate crossroads, c. 1903. This group of buildings was erected on the former village green. In the late nineteenth century, Haggate was still the main village in Briercliffe. The post office was a shop from 1870. The reading rooms to the right had been built by public subscription in 1877.

Haggate Hill End. This was originally the home of the Smith family, who were the founders of the wool and cotton industry in Briercliffe. The building was sold to the Nelson Co-operative Society in 1920 and was transformed into a guesthouse and holiday home. Famous people who have stayed here include Emmanuel Shinwell and Victor Feather who met his future wife here. Both were activists in the Labour movement.

Smallshaw, *c.* 1908. Rosegrove was an important railway centre for the Lancashire & Yorkshire Railway (LYR). Extensive sidings and an engine shed were to the left of the signal box, built in 1901. In the centre is a seventeenth-century building. To the right is a small shed housing an engine, which shunted at the Smallshaw coke ovens.

Copy Banker, 1968. The railway between Todmorden and Burnley was one of the last places where steam engines could be seen. Copy Pit was a favourite with steam enthusiasts, especially in the last few years of steam on British railways. Photographer Mike Taylor wrote: 'sunset in the Cliviger Valley as 48115 banks a loaded coal train up to Copy Pit summit on 13 June 1968'.

Bank Top Railway Station, *c.* 1922. The Benn and Cronin advertising timetable was installed for the LYR in 1921. Departure times were shown by destination. The left-hand side covered east Lancashire and Yorkshire; the right covered the Lancashire coast, Manchester and London. Sunday times were at the bottom. In the early 1900s the LYR ran at least 100 trains through the station every weekday.

Rosegrove, 21 July 1968. As at Copy Pit, the railway's steep gradient between Burnley Central and Rosegrove made it a favourite with photographers. Special excursions were frequent in 1968. Here, 70013 *Oliver Cromwell* passes through Rosegrove. The engine is preserved and will hopefully be fully restored to steam by 2008.

Molly Wood, c. 1910. Though it has gone down in folklore as where a murder was committed, the site was a popular picnic spot. People often danced here and at nearby Knotts to the sound of a concertina. In summer the stream became a 'collier's dip': it was dammed and miners washed off the dirt from the coal mine.

Lowerhouse, c. 1910. The village cricket club was founded in 1862 and has played at Liverpool Road since 1865. In 1892, the club joined the Lancashire League. Their first major trophy win was in the Worsley Cup in 2004, followed by the Lancashire League Championship in 2005.

Top Street. The street, on the south side of Finsleygate, was one of those laid out with back-to-back housing in the early 1800s. The majority of these types of houses were built before 1854 'without any sort of general plan ... the only condition seems to be they must not be built or encroach upon the highway'. Once considered 'the homes of respectable people', but later 'the despair of the town missionary and school board officer', these, and other houses, affected the death rate in the town. The houses on Top Street were demolished in the early 1920s. A few back-to-backs survive (in 2006) at Duke Bar.

Above: Burnley Cemetery. The cemetery opened in 1856 replacing older burial sites at St Peter's and other churches. There were separate burial areas for Anglicans, Catholics and Dissenters. Records show (from 1857-1877) the lowest number of yearly burials was 395, with the highest at 1,226. The average age of death was sixteen to twenty-one for men and twenty-one to twenty-four for women. The number of children who died under the age of five varied between 167 in 1858 and 630 in 1874.

Left: Memorial card. These cards became very popular in Victorian times. They were keepsakes given to family and friends. This one recorded the death of Sarah Altham of Padiham, 'who departed this life April 22 1907 aged 8 months'.

Opposite above: Padiham Road, *c.* 1911. Jubilee Chapel (left) was built in 1902. The larger houses on the right were built in stages from the late 1880s. Residents in these were from the professional classes. The horse-drawn cart is from Oak Mount Laundry.

Padiham Road, *c.* 1912. Separate communities such as Gannow Top developed in the town. The man to the left of the lamp (with the stick) is almost certainly 'Silly Jimmy' or 'Jimmy Gannow Top'. Richard Broughton, a picture-postcard specialist, took the photograph. He did not have far to travel from his Woodbine Road studio.

Padiham, *c.* 1898. The image is one half of a stereoscope photograph taken by Milford Wright, who had premises on Hollingreave Road. Despite the unusual nature of the procession – a man is on a horse, real or fake, to the left of the tram – little is known about the event.

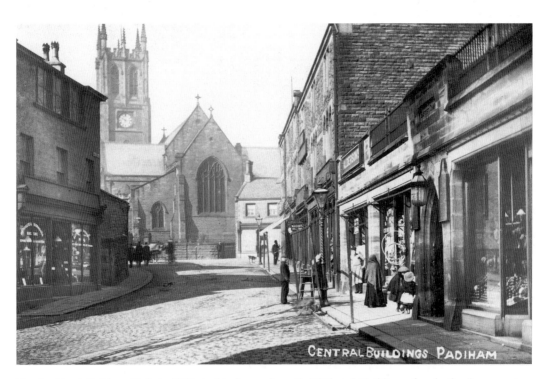

Burnley Road, Padiham. Built in 1878, the block was also called Webster's Buildings after the family who owned the butcher's shop on the corner of Moor Lane. John Alderson's shop is about to get a new window. The entrance to the Burnley Road Baptist Chapel was under the archway.

four

Work

Letterhead, 1937. Benjamin Thornber, from Rimington, established the family cotton firm in 1856. Growth was rapid in the 1870s and the business was concentrated around the canal at Daneshouse. Characteristic features included: multi-storey spinning and preparation areas, the weaving shed with a saw-tooth-shaped roof, and the engine house with an arched window and boiler house nearby.

Opposite: Kings Mill, Bridge Street. Local businessman Thomas Preston spoke to the Literary and Scientific Club in 1917. He recalled a time 'before the mills in this the Park area. The scene is quite changed since Spencer and Moore's great factory (Kings Mill) were put (built). The view across the river over the park and to the North Parade was extensive and beautiful. The steep escarpments alongside the river up and round the church brought a romance that cannot now be gratified'. Such sentiments were common in the nineteenth and early twentieth centuries. The development of the cotton industry, with spinning mills (Kings) and other industries such as the brewery to the left, dramatically altered the landscape and social development of the town. At the time of the photograph, Nuttall & Co., famous for their ready reckoners, occupied the mill.

Dinner time, Albion Mill, *c.* 1905. The aptly named Cotton Street runs across the gates. In 1912, there were nine mills in Whittlefield with several run by Robert Pickles. Their Cairo Mill is to the left of the workers who are wearing the uniform of the cotton industry. Typically this was a pair of clogs, a shawl, a waistcoat and cap. The photograph was taken from Pickles' shuttle works.

Gannow Lane. The photograph was taken from the window of Richard Broughton's studio. It was sold both as a postcard called a 'weavers' strike' – probably in 1911 – as well as a 'let's turn eaw't'. Strikes, in some cases bitter, were fairly common in the industry both locally and regionally.

Altham's, Heasandford Mill, *c.* 1908. The mill was built a few years before this photograph was taken. It was one of the first to have looms run by electricity. The company had its own fire crew. William Kershaw (far right) won several awards for saving people from the mill lodge and canal.

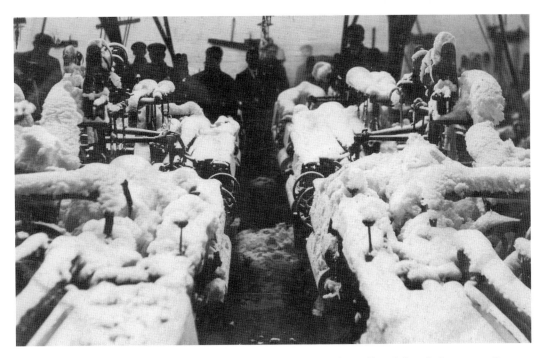

Plumbe Street shed, 29 December 1908. The blizzard seems to have affected the whole country. Over 4,000 loads of snow were collected in the town. There were large temperature fluctuations in the week. It dropped 27°F in a week then rose 25°F in two days, spoiling skaters' fun on the millponds.

Above: Mill Street, Lowerhouse. The Dugdale family developed Lowerhouse as a mill village. Originally, the firm worked a factory built in the 1790s (opposite) then concentrated the business in the 1836 mill on the right. The Dugdales built houses, a shop, a church and a canteen. One of the successful partners in the firm was Richard Shaw and because of his ability it was said by some that it was the worst thing that happened to Lowerhouse when he became the town's first MP in 1868.

Above: Lowerhouse Printworks, *c.* 1887. Daniel Drew photographed the works from Schole Bank. Alexander Drew & Sons came to Lowerhouse in 1872 and three sons were involved in the calico printing business. Daniel looked after the day-to-day running of the works. He was largely responsible for developing and expanding the factory in the 1880s.

1. The bell house.
2. Water-powered cotton mill built *c.* 1795.
3. The 'new mill', *c.* 1801. A cotton mill.
4. 'China blue house'.
5. Chimney built in 1885. This replaced an earlier chimney to the right.
6. Bleach house.
7. Machine print shop.
8. Colour house formerly used for hand block printing of cloth.
9. New printshops.
10. Engraving shop where patterns for printing machines were made.
11. The Drew family (Daniel's) home.
12. Lowerhouse farm.

Opposite below: Gatehouse, Lowerhouse Printworks, *c.* 1885. The calico printing works was one of the largest in east Lancashire and many of their products were sent to markets overseas. The gatehouse was built in 1880 as part of general improvements. The gatekeeper's responsibilities included: weighing all goods, recording the names of workers who were late, and stopping workers taking food into the factory.

Margerison's Printworks, Calder Vale, *c.* 1870. The factory was one of several calico printing works in the town that developed from the late 1700s to the early 1800s. Margerison's was the site of Burnley Paper Works, opened in 1875. Calico printing and paper used large amounts of water in their processes, so the site was ideal for paper making.

Comic card. Local holidays were taken in 'wakes weeks'. It was fairly common for people to send postcards from the town to family and friends on holiday, reminding them what they had to come back to. In this case it was weavers' tools and the weaving shed. Messages on the reverse also sometimes reflected the lifestyle of the workers.

Burnley Brick & Lime Co., 1914. The factory was built at Barden in 1876. It was intended that lime would be transported on the canal but this part of the business never developed. The works closed in 1914 to be replaced by one at Heasandford.

May Day Parade, 1926. The traditional parade had gone out of fashion. Massey's Brewery revived it on a smaller scale in 1924. A competition was organised between their different drays and a short procession followed through the town.

Boggart Bridge Pit, 17 February 1928. The colliery, off Todmorden Road, was opened in 1860. In 1866, a boiler explosion at the pit killed two workers. Fatalities when one or two miners died were fairly common in local mines. The total number of men killed in the Burnley coalfield is estimated to be over 500. The largest number of fatalities (sixty-eight) in a single accident in the coalfield was at Moorfield, Altham, in 1883.

Copy Pit. The colliery was sunk in the 1860s. It had unusual 'back-to-back' winding gear, with one engine working both shafts. As one of the cages was wound up the other one dropped. The pit, being so close to the railway, had its own sidings with a gantry passing over the road to load the railway trucks. The photograph of Copy was one of several in Cliviger made into greetings cards.

Bank Hall Colliery, *c.* 1891. Among the group of blacksmiths are the father and son pair of James and Harry Simpson (middle row, fourth and third from the left). Another son also worked at the colliery. Bank Hall was the town's biggest pit and required a large number of blacksmiths to keep it running.

Bank Hall Colliery, 1950s. The blacksmiths were responsible for repairing equipment used at the pit such as tubs, rails and fences. They tended to be a separate workforce to the miners.

Hapton Valley Colliery, 1967. The miners are, from left to right: Norman Green, Walter Shaw and John Hutchinson. John trained at Bank Hall Colliery in 1954 where his first wage was just over £2. He worked at Hapton Valley from 1960 until the early 1970s. He was underground on 22 March 1962 when an explosion occurred. John and a Polish workmate called Tony found their way to 'Joe Leach's junction' and met Horace Lister. All Horace said was 'it's gone, it's gone up'. The Hapton Valley Disaster cost the lives of nineteen miners aged between sixteen and fifty-five, including John's best friend, Bob Dunstan.

Above: Tom Sutcliffe, 1964. Tom was the third generation of Sutcliffes to run the watch-making and jewellery business at Duke Bar. Sutcliffe Sutcliffe (known as 'double Sut') founded the firm in 1868 as an offshoot of his grocery and drapers business. Tom followed his father, working from 1914-1964. He was responsible for maintaining all the clocks in the Duke Bar area. Tom took this responsibility very seriously, even returning from honeymoon to wind the clock on St Andrew's Church spire.

Right: Florence Brown, 1955. Florence was working on the Marks & Spencer payroll when this fashion photograph was taken in the boss's office. A year later, all goods at M&S stores were sold under the 'St Michael' label.

Staff at H. & R. Clegg, *c.* 1920. The firm was founded after the First World War as a shopfitters, plumbers and builders. On the far left is Robert Clegg; nearby is Rennie Clegg (wearing an apron) and smoking the pipe is Horace Clegg. In the doorway is W.B. McCourt, apprentice joiner, a later director of the firm.

Electric showroom, *c.* 1930. The Corporation showroom was opened in 1929. A bedroom was on the first floor displaying various electrical items: to some it was 'a slightly dangerous place to sleep in'. Kitchen appliances were on the second floor. In the 1930s, a fully equipped electrically run house on Kiddrow Lane could be bought for £495.

Product promoter, *c.* 1930. Parkinson's were very adept at advertising. Originally from Nelson, the manufacturing chemist was on Curzon Street. From amongst hundreds of products their most famous were pills ranging from varieties including 'female', 'head' and 'blood and stomach'. These were sold through a network of corner shops and, along with other cures, provided an alternative to doctors before the National Health Service was created. The woman is advertising castor oil, custard powder and stomach pills.

Jerry Dawson, 1930s. Jerry was a home-grown Burnley footballer. Born in Cliviger, he played 522 league games for the Clarets from 1907-1928. He missed out on the 1914 victory in the cup final but was awarded a medal in the 1920/21 championship-winning team. Apparently, he wore the medal on his watch chain.

Bicycle, 1901. John G. Coates built the powered bicycle. Originally from Leyburn, tradition has it that he went to sea and only came to Burnley to attend an inquest. He remained to set up a hardware business on Bridge Street. He was also an inventor. In a testimonial, the bicycle had 'run between 300 and 400 miles … the speed is quite up to the standard stated and on two or three occasions I have managed from 25 to 27 miles per hour'.

St James' Street, 1920s. Oddie's Café is to the right of the Palace Cinema. William H. Oddie founded the family-run bakers in Colne in 1905. The company opened and acquired premises throughout the area including Seed's Café.

Bill Clements, 1930s. Bill is pictured in the kitchen at the Savoy Café. A menu from the 1920s shows the range of dishes available, from hors d'oeuvre, au petits repas, to a lunch costing 2s with a selection of main courses including boiled codfish and roast lamb. Bill spent his working life at Oddie's. When the Savoy closed he worked in Nelson making sauces and sausages.

Henry Mozley, 1920. Henry was the general manager of the Corporation Tramways. Under him the service became the envy of many and was seen as the best in the country. He was praised for his inventions, innovations and technical know-how, as well as 'the remarkable immunity from serious accidents on the Burnley system'. His development of the Burnley bogie for trams meant that people could be carried safely and smoothly on hilly routes.

Fish seller, *c.* 1880. Photographs of Victorian and Edwardian streets often show a horse and cart. It was also common for the owner to be photographed with his cart in all its splendour, decorated for a special procession. It is less common to show one as it would have been used everyday. Mr Hitchon is the owner.

Parliament Street, 1910. Both London and Lancashire can lay claim to introducing fish-and-chip shops. The town's first chippie – usually run by a husband, wife and helper – opened in the 1880s. By 1893, there were eighty in the town. This shop opened in around 1900. John Bennett acquired the premises a few years later.

Above: Printer's proof, 1890s. The wheelwright had one of the most important trades. The carts they made were used throughout the Victorian period and well into the twentieth century, by greengrocers, fishmongers, coal and milkmen, the railway and rag-and-bone men. Horse-drawn coal and milk floats were a common sight until the 1950s.

Opposite above: Higher Ridge Farm, 1901. Helen Howker is with 'Ridge Jenny', a shire horse that won a medal at Worsthorne Agricultural Show. The terrace behind was built in 1873-4 with money from the Thursbys who were coal mine owners. These and other houses in the town were built for miners from Cornwall and Devon, who acted as strike breakers against Burnley miners.

Opposite below: Rosegrove Farm. The mixed farm, off Liverpool Road, was a typical example of a family-run business. It became known as Riddiough's Farm, after the owner. The last resident was John N. Scarisbrick, and when the building was demolished in 1976 to make way for the motorway it was still lit by gas.

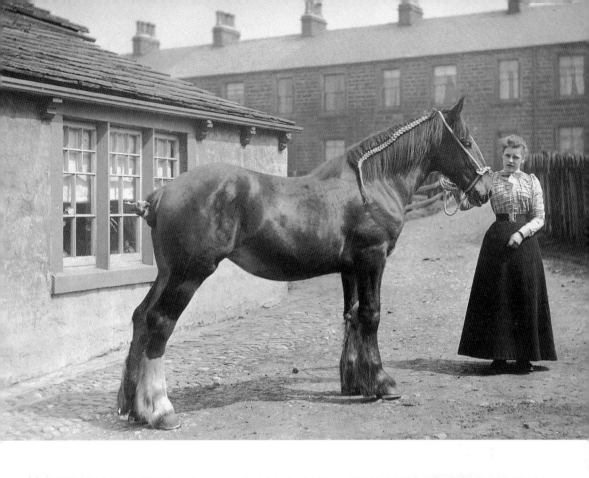

ROSEGROVE. FARM.

Conservatory, Thompson Park, *c.* 1962. The conservatory was near the main entrance and was a popular attraction. The main planting was in the centre with other pot plants on staging around the side. David Nield is tending the tropical and semi-tropical plants. He went on to study horticulture at the Yorkshire College of Agriculture.

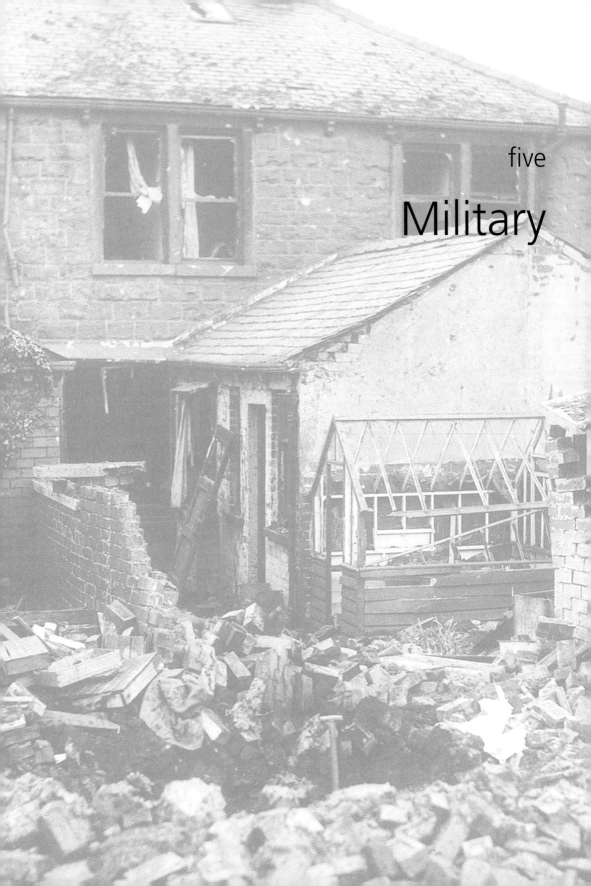

David Duncan, *c.* 1880. David served in the 59th Regiment of Foot with the rank of Warrant Officer II. He fought in Afghanistan and was awarded the Queen's Afghanistan medal (which he is wearing) with the clasp 'Ahmed Khel'. The old Regiments of Foot were re-designated in 1881. The 59th became the 2nd Battalion East Lancashire Regiment (ELR). David served in the ELR as did both his sons who were killed in the First World War.

Right: Presenting the colours, 18 June 1907. The local militia (5th Royal Lancashire Militia) was formed in the 1850s. Caroline, wife of Colonel Charles Towneley, had made one of these colours. They were presented at St Peter's Church on the eighty-second anniversary of the Battle of Waterloo, and a year before the Territorial Force was formed.

Below: Bank Parade, 1909. The march was held shortly after the national formation of the Territorial Force. Territorials were part-time soldiers providing additional home defence. Burnley's was the 5th Battalion ELR. Their drill hall was at Keighley Green. A few years after this photograph was taken, two territorial battalions served heroically in the war. How many of these boys joined them?

Shooting team, 1912. These men from 'C' Company ELR Territorials won the Corporation Challenge Shield. Pictured are, from left to right, back: Joseph Sugden, E. and T. Hewitson, W. Halstead, Thomas Thornton, R. Taylor. Sitting: P. Nessler, Henry Bolton, Harry Jobling, ? Scott. Front: George Haffner, E. Berry. Halstead and Scott are wearing campaign medals from the Boer War. Colour Sergeant Nessler is wearing the army service and good conduct medal. Of these men, Sugden, Thornton and Bolton were killed in the First World War. Haffner and Jobling were wounded.

A. Victor Smith. Victor was the son of the town's chief constable. He served in the ELR and his act of self-sacrifice on 23 December 1915 led to the award of the Victoria Cross (VC). A grenade slipped from his hand 'but seeing that the officers and men were unable to get into cover he flung himself down upon it. He was instantly killed. His magnificent act of self-sacrifice undoubtedly saved many lives'. His VC is displayed in Towneley Hall.

Thomas Whitham. Thomas was born in Worsthorne and he served in the Coldstream Guards. He was awarded the Victoria Cross for disabling a German machine gun in the third Battle of Ypres, 1917. Burnley people presented him with a gold watch and he received a clock from people in Worsthorne. Unfortunately, Thomas fell on hard times after the war and he pawned the VC and watch. He died in 1924 and was buried with full military honours in the Inghamite burial ground, Fence. The VC and watch were bought by the Corporation from the pawnbroker and presented to Towneley Hall. They are displayed at Towneley. Worsthorne Parish Council gave the clock to the museum in 1981.

Officers, Cairo, 1915. The group, 1/5 Battalion ELR, embarked for Gallipoli in May 1915. A month later six were dead. One died in France in 1917. They include the Bolton brothers and Alan Rodgers. Henry Bolton (middle, fifth from left) and brother John (back, fourth from right) were killed within a few days of each other. Alan (back right) lived on Scott Park Road with his mother and father Robert (front, third from right). Robert wrote to his wife: 'Alan still missing. No news. Fear the worst. Am well'. Alan's body was never found.

Opposite: Ernest Ogle, *c.* 1915. Ernest (seated) served in the Royal Garrison Artillery. He was killed in action on the same day as his parents' silver wedding anniversary. A chaplain wrote to his mother: 'It is with a heavy heart that I write informing you of the death of your son … I am very sorry for you … may the God of all consolation be near you in this hour of bitter sorrow that hides your heart … PS your boy is buried in a well-kept cemetery'. The cemetery, Westhof Farm in Belgium, is one of the smaller ones tended by the Commonwealth War Graves Commission.

Left: Mrs Sutcliffe, 1917. She was 'doing her little bit' for the war effort. Families and friends sent parcels to men on active service. On one occasion, a food parcel addressed to Harry Stanworth arrived too late for him to use. Harry had been killed. The food was divided among members of his platoon. The wrapping from the parcel was sent back to his parents with the word 'killed' and the date of death written on it.

Below: Amy Foster. Pictured with 'Bomber' (left) and 'Twig', Amy was one of several local children who collected money in the First World War. She was known as 'Hieland Lassie'. Her first kilt was home made. The money she collected bought food, cigarettes and notepaper for troops overseas. Amy also raised money for St Dunstan's, London, a workshop and home for servicemen who had been blinded.

War memorial, *c.* 1930. Several designs were considered for the memorial until one was accepted from artist Walter Gilbert from Birmingham. The three main figures represent the navy, army and air force. Walter described the memorial to be 'a cenotaph in form (and is) a visible expression of the emotion felt in the human heart for the deeds of those who have fallen. The mother (left), overwhelmed with emotion, places a wreath in the memory of her son at the foot of the Cenotaph, and as she bends down the Cenotaph shapes itself in her heart with the features of her son. By the side of the mother and touching her is the rosemary bush for remembrance and under the rosemary is the cricket bat and the ball for the son is the boy to the mother always – the son who never grows up in her eyes. To the sister or wife (right) bringing garlands and the palm of victory, the memory of the courage and the prowess of the man fills their hearts. They rejoice with shining hearts that their man was a man among men'.

Over 4,000 Burnley men died in the war – about eight per cent of the total male population, or about twelve per cent of men of serviceable age. This was one of the largest percentages for the whole country.

ARP wardens, 1941. The three men (who are, from left to right: Harry Haffner, George Dunkerley and William Lancaster) filmed an air-raid precautions exercise. The film starts in the central control at Daneshouse. Wardens in Burnley Wood make sure people are in the air-raid shelter, fire fighters put out an incendiary bomb and an ambulance transports people to hospital. At the all clear, wardens enjoy a well-earned mug of tea.

Opposite: War memorial, Brooklands Chapel, 1920s. Unveiled in 1923, the memorial reflected the connection with the Yorkshire Dales. Of the eighteen names, six were descended from Swaledale families with nearly all living in Burnley Wood. John Reynoldson was the chapel's organist. In his memory his father, James, wrote music to the words of an old Methodist hymn that was published as a postcard. Proceeds from the sale of 'Gunnerside' went to the National Children's Home. The hymn is occasionally played and sung in the Dales. When James returned to live in Gunnerside he named his cottage 'Brooklands'. The original postcard was printed the wrong way round.

Above: Civil defence, *c.* 1940. Because of the fear of a gas attack in the war all people had to carry a gas mask. The group is outside No. 9 Ladbrooke Grove. They are, from left to right: Florence Porrett, Edna Greenwood, Rhoda Howker, Margaret Gutteridge and Evelyn Walmsley. The photograph was probably taken as a joke on their part. The women served in the ARP control room at a mill in Daneshouse.

Left: Eric Anderson, May 1944. Local cinemas, theatres and the wireless played a great part in keeping people's morale high. Walt Disney made *Victory Through Air Power*. The film suggested that bombing cities was the best way to defeat the enemy.

Bomb damage, 1941. The house, No. 439 Rossendale Road, was damaged by a German air attack in May. The photograph was published in the *Burnley Express* but was only referred to as being in the north west. Burnley was not heavily bombed but the Germans had identified the main targets including Rosegrove railway yard, the gas works, canal and industrial areas.

155 Light Anti-Aircraft Battery, North Africa, December 1940. The territorial battery was raised locally and served with distinction in France and North Africa. It is thought that the unit had been in action when the photograph was taken. Johnny Wearden (left) won a Military Medal (he was recommended for a Distinguished Conduct Medal) when he directed the anti-aircraft gun 'against AFVs (armoured fighting vehicles) and inf. (infantry) with great speed and precision'. Anti-aircraft guns were used with devastating effects against armoured vehicles, particularly in North Africa. To the far right is Bill Jenkins.

Doris and Doreen Wellock, 1940s. Alfred, husband of Doris and father of Doreen, served in the Royal Artillery. He carried a photograph of his wife and daughter off to war. Alfred was captured by the Germans and interned in a prisoner-of-war camp. A fellow prisoner painted this picture based on the photograph. After Alfred's unfortunate death in the camp, the photograph and painting were returned to the family on Stanworth Street.

Prisoners of war reunion, 1963. The group of ex-RAF men met at the Odeon Cinema. From left to right, back row: Edward Bellis, Alan Thornton, George Horn, Jack Wotherspoon, Richard Ashworth, Walter Sharp, Ronald Carter. Second row: Mr Jones (Odeon), James Hutchinson. Third row: Philip Daulby, the Mayor and Mayoress, J. Cakebread. Front row: Thomas Clucas, Lawrence Bone, Wilfred Marshall. Each had their own story, some a harrowing one, of their capture and imprisonment. George Horn saved his own and two comrades' lives with his father's police whistle. He used it to attract the attention of Italian sailors on a passing ship after he was shot down in the Mediterranean. Thomas Clucas endured a walk through the desert when his bomber crashed because of mechanical failure.

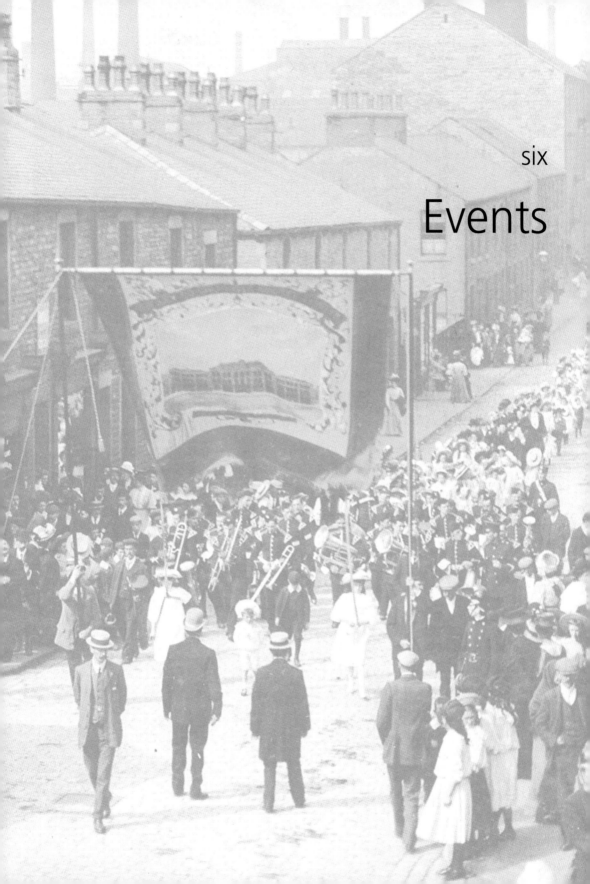

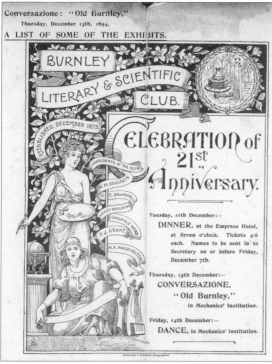

Conversazione: "Old Burnley,"
Thursday, December 13th, 1894.
A LIST OF SOME OF THE EXHIBITS.

Above: St John the Baptist Church, 25 April 1891. The church had been built in 1880 largely because of benefactors Lady Scarlett (wife of the hero of the Crimean War) and the Thursby family. The tower was added in 1891, its 'stone being laid with due Masonic rite by Brother J.O.S. Thursby in the name of the Great Architect of the Universe'.

Left: Programme, 1894. The Literary and Scientific Club's Conversazione saw it display various items on the theme of 'Old Burnley'. These included a collection of pattern books from Margerison's (see p.54), part of the stocks (see p.18), photographs, paintings, deeds and manuscripts. The club's presidents were influential in medicine, literature, publishing and finance.

Scholarship students, 1898-1903. One of the reasons for an improvement in education was the work of teachers such as Ernest Evans. Pictured are, from left to right, back: William Rawson, T. Keegan, Bernard O'Shaughnessy, G. and J. Haworth, Thomas Southwell, A. Pickles, F. Thistlethwaite, Tobias Clegg, T. Thornton, Ernest Evans, William Luty, Alfred Eastwood, Charles Martin, T. Dewhurst, Florence Pratt, Ethel Mellor. Under Ernest's tutorship – he himself had humble beginnings – his pupils from the Technical School won national scholarships year after year, many in science. Thomas Southwell became a world authority on parasitology. Ethel Mellor worked as a cotton weaver before graduating from the Royal College of Science, London in 1906. She was the first woman to be granted a doctorate (in science) from Paris University in 1922. She was also an associate of London's Royal College.

Mr. WILLIAM A ARMOUR'S COMPANY

WHAT A WOMAN DID!

Act II Scene II "You're intoxicated Fritz!"

GAIETY THEATRE BURNLEY, Monday, Jan 1st, 1906, and during the Week.

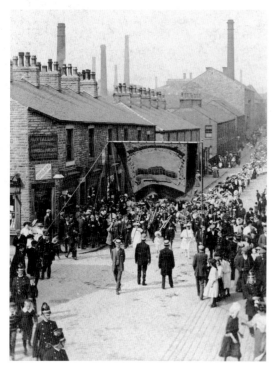

Above: Advertisement, 1906. Before purpose-built theatres, plays were performed in pubs. One such was *Othello* at the Hall Inn in 1814. The wooden-built Gaiety opened in 1880. It was known as the 'blood tub … where lurid dramas were played weekly. Nearly all the patrons bought bottles of stout, chips and fish, pies … and fighting was a common sight'.

Left: Co-op procession, Plumbe Street. Apart from the retail business the Co-op was involved with the welfare of its members. The movement ran insurance, funeral, education, pension and house-building schemes. It encouraged better rights for women. Rambles and day trips were organised and thousands of people were attracted to the annual fete and procession.

Dan Irving, Market Street, *c.* 1918. Dan was born in Birmingham and he came to Burnley as secretary of the Marxist Social Democratic Federation (SDF). He was elected as a Labour councillor in 1902 and became the town's first Labour MP in 1918. Some of his campaign speeches were given from exactly the same place on Market Street as H.M. Hyndman's (leader of the SDF) a few years before. His election card for 1923 reflected the time: 'yes we have no bananas … we have no enjoyment on doles and unemployment, yes we have no bananas but we're voting for Irving today'. He successfully defended the seat.

Wedding of William Greenwood and Mary Steele, 1 August 1907. Mary's dress and hat were borrowed from her parents' employers. The locket had, and still has, a photograph of the couple. Mary attended St Andrew's Church all her life but the couple were married in William's church, in the Ebenezer Baptist Chapel. The couple's first three children died young.

Wedding of A. Sidney Edwards and Lily Whewell, 7 July 1920. Sid told his landlady he had seen 'the girl I'm going to marry' in Scott Park. He only found out who the girl, Lily, was after being formally introduced. Their marriage was deferred because of the First World War. During the war, Sid carried a photograph of Lily with him. He was wounded in action on 1 July 1916 while serving in the Accrington Pals when a shell splinter narrowly missed his brain.

Wedding of Cyril B. Spencer and Maria E. Grant, 30 December 1915. Maria had promised to marry Cyril before the end of 1915 – they just made it. The couple made their first home at No. 146 Coal Clough Lane and were parents to Philip (who died in South Africa in the Second World War) and Kenrick (Ken). Philip was a brilliant scholar. He was educated locally then at Richmond and St John's College, Oxford. While in South Africa he wrote an essay on the injustice of apartheid. Fortune Press, who had published works by such people as Philip Larkin and Dylan Thomas, also issued some of Philip's poems. Ken became a national authority on the lapwing and an expert on local history. Also pictured are, from left to right: Bert Grant, Kathrine Spencer (front), and William and Gertrude Grant.

Wedding of Frank Howarth and Nellie Clark, 8 July 1933. The couple were married in St Andrew's Church. Frank had his own saddlers business on Yorkshire Street. Their first child died four days after he was born. After the war, the couple adopted a baby girl. A letter sent to them said that 'if you choose her you may be able to take her, therefore please bring a shawl, nappy and safety pin, suitcase for clothing and leave your cot in readiness'.

Wedding of Harry Swain and Edith Catlow, 18 September 1943. The couple made their home in Harold Street. Harry was killed in action in March 1945, serving in the Cameronians. He is buried, along with 7,000 others, in the Reichswald War Cemetery. Also pictured are, from left to right: Fred Lawson, Mildred Catlow, Joseph Watson, Elsie Catlow, Gilbert Harrison and Marjorie Swain (young girl).

Above: Wedding of David Hewitson and Jean Eastwood, 3 January 1959. The couple were married in St John's Church, Gannow. Their reception was held at the Mitre pub followed by a four-day honeymoon in London. David studied architecture at university but unfortunately died in 1964. Also pictured are, from left to right, front: Brenda Heild, Elizabeth (Betty) Eastwood and Jean Wild.

Right: Wedding of Harry Newsham and Rosalie Moorhouse, 13 May 1967. Harry and Rosalie met at the Locarno Ballroom (a popular meeting place) and were married in the registry office nine months later. Rosalie's dress and shoes cost £6. A three-course reception, consisting of soup, beef, trifle and two bottles of wine, was held at Storey's, Harle Syke. The total cost of the wedding was £111.

BALLOON AND PARACHUTE ASCENDING FROM ATHLETIC GRO AT THE FLOWER SHOW BURNLEY. AUG 22 1908.

Left: Balloon flight, 22 August 1908. A flower show was revived in 1907 and held again the following year. Children were encouraged to take part by growing small plants. The show produced a 'remarkable wealth of blooms'. The balloon flight seems to have gone largely unreported.

Below: Mitella Street, November 1931. After heavy rain, Fulledge was prone to flooding. The river Calder had burst its banks and, despite hardship for the poultry farmers, there were some more humorous moments when residents could only reach the town centre by walking on the top of garden walls!

Opposite below: Royal visit, 1955. The Queen and Duke of Edinburgh spent a short time in Burnley on their visit to local towns. The women's section of the British Legion is outside their headquarters on Richard Street. Over 5,000 people paid to see the Queen and Duke of Edinburgh's signatures, which raised over £127 for the Mayor's fund.

Mosley Heights, 1950. Walter Bennett (right) directed the excavation of the Bronze Age
burial mound. The site was one of the first 'rescue' digs in Lancashire. The finds included three
cremations in urns. Recent research in 2005 has found that the first of these belonged to an adult
in their early twenties. Bodies in two of the urns contained offerings of chert (used for arrow
making) and galena. Analysis of charcoal suggests the area was covered in mature oak forest.

Above: Merrie England, 1961. The production was part of the borough's centenary celebrations. The 'Four Men of Windsor' were: the butler played by Alex Ingham, baker James Halstead, tinker William Beswick, and the tailor played by Richard Lewis.

Left: Centenary carnival, 1961. The procession started at Park Lane and finished at Casterton Avenue. Many organisations and businesses were involved. Henry Whitaker, clog dancer from Nelson, dressed up as 'Old Mother Riley'. He raised thousands of pounds for charities in this outfit. Henry put his agility and fitness down to a diet of milk, water, eggs, fruit, nuts and vegetables.

seven

'Characters'

THE GOOD OLD TIMES ARE DEAD AND GONE,

A NEW LOCAL BALLAD AS SUNG BY JOHN OTTERMUCK,

DESCRIPTIVE OF DAYS GONE BY.

Chance having thrown so many eccentrick heroes into one hostel and John being unanimously called upon for a song, we cannot resist placing the picture entire before the public.

TOM SHEW, (CHAIRMAN,) a Philosopher,

Tom Testy - - -	A POLITICIAN,	The two Johns - - -	TINNERS,
Brown - - - -	A WISEACRE,	Noisy Neddy - - - -	A BELLMAN,
Childers - - - -	A CHURCH BEADLE,	Frank - - - - - -	A BROTHER,
Soapy Tom - - -	A BARBER,	Old Duke - - - - -	A SLINKER,

Tamarind Jerry - - - a Lady's quack Patentee, proprietor and inventor of the Celebrated Wellington Wafers, Elixer of Red Cabbage and Syrup of Raisen Stalks.---

Songsheet. Part of the ballad, written *c.* 1856, is shown. Local people, events and places are mentioned and it is clear that these were not all good old times. The 'characters' mentioned include bellman Edward Robinson (Noisy Neddy), chemist J.J. Smith (Tamarind Jerry), and John Taylor (John Ottermuck). Some of the people mentioned in the remainder of the ballad had died but were still remembered. Similarly events, such as the collapse of Holgate's bank in 1824, were not forgotten: it 'tun'd tradesmen upside down … the shuttle then was dull'.

CHARLES OWEN.

Born 1809. Died 1869

Charles Owen. In the nineteenth century he led discussion groups – 'a coffee house babble' – on free will, suffrage, socialism and improved water supply to combat poor public health. He led a public outcry in 1857 when Charles Towneley closed the 'Rabbit Walk' across Towneley Park. A poster was published, savagely criticising Towneley. Both the walk and a crossing over the river Calder were reopened in 1858.

RICHARD SIMPSON.
DIED. 1881.   AGE 99

Richard Simpson, *c.* 1880. It was written, a hundred years later, that 'they seemed to cherish characters more than we do in our permissive society'. These people were well known, not in terms of derision but by familiarity and affection. Richard, who died in 1881 aged ninety-nine, was the last person in town to wear traditional knee britches.

Robert Mosley Master, *c.* 1862. Robert was probably the greatest of all ministers in the town. During his incumbency at St Peter's he established six 'daughter' churches and oversaw the founding of the St Peter's and Pickup Croft Schools, as well as changes inside the church. He was known as the 'clogging parson' because he set up a fund to provide clogs for poorer children.

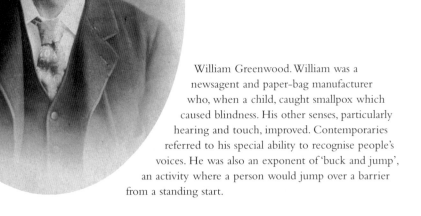

William Greenwood. William was a newsagent and paper-bag manufacturer who, when a child, caught smallpox which caused blindness. His other senses, particularly hearing and touch, improved. Contemporaries referred to his special ability to recognise people's voices. He was also an exponent of 'buck and jump', an activity where a person would jump over a barrier from a standing start.

Johnny and Jane Thompson. In the 1880s the couple were working in a cotton mill in the town centre and would walk to work from Worsthorne. They then became hawkers, selling from a cart pulled by a donkey. Apparently they could sing, on request, anything from the Methodist hymnbook. Johnny died in 1898 and was buried in the Wesleyan Chapel churchyard, Worsthorne.

John Pollard. Described in 1901 as probably the oldest bell ringer in the country, he first rang the bells at St Peter's in 1837. He 'rang at the occasion of the Queen's coronation, marriage and death… (and) has rung the old year out and the new one in every year during her reign'. John died in 1902 of 'senile decay'.

Above: Tattersall Wilkinson. 'The Sage of Roggerham' (wearing the fez) was probably the most famous local 'character'. He was almost a legend in his own life despite spending much of it away from the area. Returning in 1884, his writings and lectures on local history, folklore, astronomy and archaeology remain relevant today. But it is only in recent years that his story has been reassessed. To the left of the door is Peter Shackleton.

Left: Peter Shackleton, 1916. Peter, who always seemed to wear a navy cap, 'had eccentric habits and peculiar tendencies'. He was a collector of curios and his gardens, first at Bankhouse then at Rectory Road, were very unusual. He collected birds, most of which had been shot. Peter wrote: '1872 snipe shot in Hapton. Grey back'd gull shot by my father near Burnley printworks stuffed by David Mitchell'.

Right: Elizabeth Harrison, 1908. 'Lady' Harrison always wore 'a large hat, lace curtain material and sometimes brown paper around her ankles. She would frequently walk to Manchester Road station – rumours had it she was waiting for the arrival of her sweetheart'. Her great grandson was Dr Michael Harrison, who was known at school as 'trammy Harry' because of his interest in transport.

Below: 'Old Barwise'. Joseph Barwise (second from right) specialised in growing dahlias. He had a nursery off Todmorden Road, south of Towneley. Joseph was the first grower from the north to win a gold medal for his dahlia 'Fortune' in 1938. He won many prizes for dahlias with local names such as 'Whalley', 'Reedley' and 'Towneley'. The National Dahlia Society's J.F. Barwise Perpetual Challenge Cup for small decoratives was named after him.

Maurice Tate, 1957. Maurice was born in 1926. He showed promise as a goalkeeper and played for Burnley FC reserves. On leaving school he started work as an apprentice steeplejack. Wearing his characteristic woolly cap he demolished many factory chimneys and buildings in the town. He felt 'safer up there than walking the streets'. Maurice died in 2001.

'Oops', Peel Mill, 1964. Maurice Tate proved he could land a chimney on 'a half crown' by dropping the chimney – as a publicity stunt – onto an old Morris Minor van. In the early 1900s there were hundreds of factory chimneys serving mills, breweries, tanneries, and iron and brick works. Demolition of these was encouraged in the 1960s, finally signifying the end of 'King Cotton'.

eight

Children

Left: Children, *c.* 1870. The original photograph is an ambrotype – a process that reduced the cost of photographs. These were popular from the mid-nineteenth century until about 1880. A glass negative image was placed in front of a black background. The resulting positive image was often fixed in a special keepsake case.

Below: Lowerhouse Printworks, 1883. The children are from the Drew family. Two of the three brothers ran the works with the third based in Manchester. Daniel Drew lived in the centre of the works with one of his brothers at Holme Lodge, Rosegrove. As the children were growing, they sailed in small boats on the large lodges and helped out at harvest time.

Daniel Drew and children, 1880s. The family (with Rab the dog) were privileged to have their own garden in Lowerhouse. There was a tennis court, a large wooden toy boat, a playhouse, seating, a hammock (Dad is in it, Mum's behind the tree), and green fields beyond. However, they also had to contend with the company gas works and the factory's smoke and smells.

School trip, c. 1890. Albert Alston's School opened on Grimshaw Street in 1887. Children were educated here until the age of thirteen. Those over thirteen could study business, journalism, banking, shorthand and 'calligraphic art'. The school opened daily, from 6-9 p.m. in the evening, and was open from 9-6 p.m. on Saturday.

Burnley Wood School, early 1900s. The school, run by the local education board, was opened in 1892 and extended in 1904. While closing time seems a free-for-all with many a smile on faces, entry into school was governed by the school signal. Children had to walk into school 'in time' with a wooden device which a teacher 'clicked'. Such signals were in use in local schools well into the 1930s.

Above: St John's Church, Cliviger, *c.* 1910. This was a popular postcard. If a card was relevant to the sender, 'x' often marked the spot. The message on this card reads, 'this is for uncall George this is were uncall Jim is put to rest at that side as I put a cross hoping you are keeping well and warking'. It is difficult to determine who 'Jim' was as the sender is not identified, but he could be a member of the Hitchon family of architects.

Right: Haytime, Cliviger, *c.* 1926. Stanley Earnshaw (left) and Fred Pickup are about to enjoy some well-earned refreshment, possibly of the herbal drink St Ora. The adults would have something stronger. Haytime was an important social event before mechanisation came to farming. Many people and families would help gather the hay during dry weather.

Heasandford. The walk along the banks of the river Brun – still enjoyed today – led to Briercliffe, Rowley and beyond Worsthorne and Boulsworth. The photograph was published as a postcard entitled 'The Great Tiddler Hunt'. Fish caught in the 1930s included trout, sticklebacks and 'tommies' (which were stone loach).

Overtown, c. 1908. The settlement was the second largest in Cliviger in the early 1800s. The community relied on farming and handloom weaving. In the 1820s a canal was planned through here, linking the Leeds–Liverpool in Burnley with the Rochdale Canal at Walsden. It is thought the girl on the right became Mrs Pimm in later life.

Above and below: Habergham festival, 23 May 1908. The festival was revived largely through the work of the Revd Thomas Williams, pictured right (see also Burnley volume one), curate of All Saints' Church, Habergham. Thomas involved himself with many social concerns and work with the unemployed. A procession involving, among others, the Church Lads' Brigade, the 'Village Terrors Band', St John Ambulance, Friar Tuck and Dick Whittington, went to Gawthorpe. Alice Duxbury was crowned May Queen.

Above: Hest Bank Camp, 1920s. A holiday camp was opened in 1926 largely due to the work of Mayor Dr J.W. Clegg. Children were taken to a camp of dormitories, a dining and school room, and a kitchen. The first group to visit consisted of twenty-five girls aged twelve to fourteen. Most of their stay was taken up with walking and playing on the beach. It was reported that they had 'not seen the sea before and their most novel experience was having a bed each'.

Left: Carnival, 1934. Bert Blackburn is holding Nancy. She is pulling Bert's replica fish cart made for him when he was four years old. The cart was used at many local fairs and carnivals. Bert became the third generation of the family to run the fish-selling business that started in 1880. He used the full-sized cart, then sold fish from a van, and finally retired in 1980. The replica cart is in the Towneley Hall collections.

Above: Accrington Road Nursery, 1936. When opened in 1932, this was one of only forty-four nurseries in the country run by a local authority. Medical and dental inspection was regular: out of fifty-six four year olds five per cent had 'unsaveable' teeth (in 2001–02 it was just over two per cent). It was thought children who attended would gain in self-confidence, intelligence and learn how to use cutlery.

Right: Richard Harvey Morgan. At St Augustine's School in 1946, pupils were asked to write an essay about memories. Ten-year-old Richard wrote about playing marbles, a hen pen, the Second World War and Paul, who 'can pee right up the wall. He sometimes gives me his chewing gum. After he has finished with it … Mr Spencer who lives next door was caught by the Japs. He looked like all bones in a brown suit when he came home'.

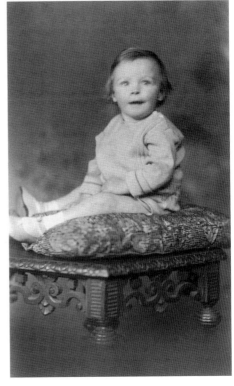

Street party, June 1953. To celebrate Queen Elizabeth's Coronation, parties were held throughout the town. This one was at the rear of Cemetery Road, Padiham. Looking towards West View Terrace, Potter's Meadow is in the background. On the menu were sandwiches, buns, jelly, blancmange, and boiled sweets washed down with Hills and Padiham aerated mineral waters. Live television coverage boosted the sales of televisions. Many of those people who were lucky enough to have a television invited neighbours into their home to watch the event.

Opposite above: Street game, 1950s. Sam Hanna photographed and filmed the game of 'weight coming on' near Beverley Street. It involved children leapfrogging onto a line of backs. This would collapse under the weight coming on. Most of the boys attended Abel Street School where Sam taught. Sam was well known for filming disappearing crafts such as clog making, charcoal burning, rush seat making and coopering.

Opposite below: Padiham, ash pad, *c.* 1955. The boys, from left to right, are: Ian Thompson, Derek Wood, Roy Kay, Duncan Armstrong and Peter Bradshaw. They were pictured on their way home from Cross Bank School. The path, from Cardwell Street towards the railway station, was probably laid out by the LYR. Originally made with ash, now concrete, the old nickname remains.

Left: Festival of Britain, June 1951. The town staged its own celebrations, with exhibitions, galas, sport, shows and theatre. The high school for girls staged *The Towneleys at Home*, with re-enactments from the family's history including Catholic persecution and the Civil War. The pupils also gave tours of the hall.

Below: Stoneyholme Recreation Ground, 1960s. Relatively few homes had gardens. Allotments, smallholdings and hen pens, and parks and recreation grounds provided open spaces. Most areas had a 'rec' as an open space and where games were played. Often, children themselves created these: 'we would use an old picking stick to hit a tin can as far as we could'.

Retirement of Ruby Mackay, 1958. Ruby worked for a total of thirty-seven years (thirty-one as head) at the Open Air School in Thompson Park. The school was opened in 1918. In the 1930s children were placed here with ailments ranging from chronic bronchitis to peritonitis. Richard Harvey Morgan (see p.113) attended because of his 'failure to thrive'. Ruby was presented with bouquets, chocolates, a wall decoration, clock and travelling bag. Pictured are, from back left to right: Freda Bartram, Mr Salisbury, Michael Roberts, Barry Salmon, Mrs Waterworth, Michael Barker, Harold Pickles, Miss Shoesmith, Marion Davies, Kathleen Kennerley, Trudy Shaw, and Ruby and Barbara Thompson.

Burnley Lads' Club football team, 1915. The club for working-class boys was founded in the early 1900s. Emphasis was placed on sport, teamwork, reading and education. The football team was runner-up in the Willie Holt Cup. Pictured are, from left to right, back row: W. Ingham, J. Sullivan, F. Whitaker, P. Barker. Middle: R. Routh, Joe Charters, Fred Metcalfe, J. Emmott, V. Briggs, E. Williams, W. Varley. Front: Harry Routh, Harry Blythe, J. Crossley, S. Wilson, A. Clegg, and Arthur Isherwood, aged fifteen.

nine

Bert's Snaps

Albert (always known as Bert) and Donald Sturgeon, c. 1926. Bert Sturgeon was born in Essex. Why he came to Burnley is a mystery. He married Clara Steele in 1920 and Donald was born in 1922. As in many family photographs, the young child features heavily. Bert printed his own photographs and experimented with different photographic techniques.

Springhill, c. 1924. Keeping hens was more than a hobby. It was an important addition to people's income and livelihoods. In 1914, a Burnley hen broke the world record for laying eggs – 284 in a year. In the 1930s, there were regular 'egg weeks' when eggs were given to the Victoria Hospital (22,000 in 1939). Similar weeks included Rat Week when, under the Rats and Mice (Destruction) Act, hundreds of rats and mice were killed.

Bert, 1921. As a young man, Bert saw himself as 'a poor little weakling, a useless ornament. I often visited music halls and became interested in the strong arm turns'. His athleticism developed while serving in the army in the First World War. He had his own strong arm act called 'Victor and Viola'.

'Leaguers', late 1920s. Bert was a 'Health and Strength Leaguer'. Members of the movement – leaguers – staged physical feats for audiences. Bert was instructor to these girls who were members of the Burnley Lane Physical Cultural Society. Demonstrations included self-defence and 'a novelty means of performing exercises to keep fit to the words and music provided by a gramophone'.

Left: Donald, *c.* 1928. Wooden and iron hoops required skill and dexterity in order to roll them, especially on cobbled streets or setts. Apparently, many wooden hoops ended up on the arms of gas lamps. Outdoor play relied on imagination as many of the toys and games were home-made.

Below: Thompson Park. The park was opened in 1930. In common with other parks it was built and developed because of a public benefactor. Thompson was more 'municipal' than other parks in the town, complete with a boating lake, Italian garden, café and large children's play area.

Above: Odeon Cinema, 1949. The cinema, built on the site of a cotton mill and opened in 1937, was the largest in town. It included air conditioning, 'deaf aids', 2,200 seats and a floodlit car park. The first main feature was *The Plainsman*. The last was *Language of Love*. On the right is the Culvert Garage with 'Ruth's' ice cream car far right.

Right: Odeon Cinema. Bert was a masseur, printer, and novelist writing such books as *The Human Mole* and *The Cranbrook Murder Mystery*. But he 'never had a very startling career'. He had a number of jobs including being a handyman at the Odeon. Colleagues at the Odeon included Frank Tipping as well as Eric Anderson (see p.80) who was one of the projectionists. Eric remembers Bert as a quiet, modest, intelligent man who was skilled at woodworking and sign writing. The pair made many of the props and advertisements used in the cinema.

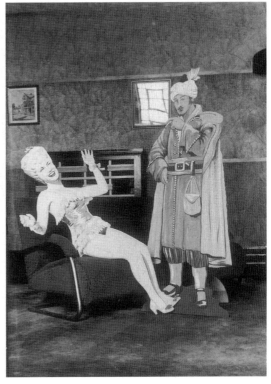

Left: Odeon staff, *c.* 1949. The group is pictured by the canal bank. They are, from left to right: Doreen Booth, Monica Tozer, Alan Entwistle, Lily Spencer and Connie Daley. Doreen was the sweet and ice cream seller; Alan was the doorman and cleaner. Monica, Lily and Connie were usherettes. Before they went on duty all had to be inspected to see if they were presentable. Monica married Eric Anderson in 1951.

Below: Lane Bottom. Behind the car is Hill Factory. This was built in 1777 as a loom shop for woollen handloom weavers. The factory was demolished in the late 1960s. At the side was a well and privies used by the people in Lane Bottom.

Clara Sturgeon, Patten Street, 1950s. The kitchen was probably the most important room. It doubled as a bathroom when tin baths were used in front of the cast-iron range. The range was used to cook on as well as to provide heat. The house and the range were kept impeccably clean.

Left: Patten Street, 1950s. There was little traffic on the streets at this time, making it fairly safe for these girls (unknown) to play out. Street games of the time included 'clog-sparking', which involved flicking the heel of your clogs on setts, 'top and whip', skipping, hopscotch and sledging down the steep and long Albion Street.

Below: Rear of Patten Street/ Gresham Place, *c.* 1948. Some of the houses have an air-raid shelter and slop water closet in the back yard. The 'long drop' toilet was in the yard and it was flushed with a 'tippler'. A rocking ceramic container was underground near the pedestal. Water from the kitchen sink (slop stone) or a grate filled the container that tipped when full. The onrush of water created the flush..

Patten Street, 1950s. The street, laid out in around 1860, was probably named after the Lancashire MP J. Wilson Patten. It ran uphill from Trafalgar Street to the railway. Typically, the road surface was granite setts, many of which still survive in the town under tarmac. The children are about to enjoy an ice cream. Patten Street was one of those demolished to make way for the Trafalgar Flats, completed in 1968. The flats themselves were demolished in 1997. Time marches on…

Other local titles published by Tempus

Accrington
JOHN GODDARD

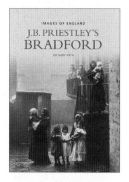

This personal selection of 200 photographs portrays some of the changes – both physical, social and cultural – that took place in Accrington during the twentieth century. Many of the events depicted here will be in the living memory of older local people. For younger Accringtonians they will reveal the world in which their parents and grandparents lived. For newcomers to the town they will arouse an interest in the history and development of their adopted home

0-7524-0376-1

J.B. Priestley's Bradford
DR GARY FIRTH

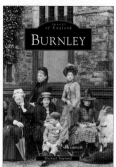

Through a selection of over 200 contemporary photographs, this book examines the influences of Edwardian Bradford which were at work upon J.B. Priestley in his most formative years, 1894–1914. We are given an insight into the pre-First World War Bradford way of life in which Gary Firth reveals a vivid, if transient, understanding of a great writer's 'lost world' – and so it was, for Priestley's early life coincided with the zenith of Bradford's golden age as a classic nineteenth-century provincial town

0-7524-3865-4

Burnley
MICHAEL TOWNEND

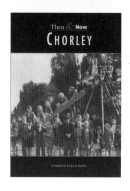

This historic array of old photographs of Burnley has been selected by the author from the extensive collection held at Towneley Hall Art Gallery and Museum. The images illustrate some of the many changes that have taken place between 1850 and 1960 in the town. Local characters are documented, including the 'demon cyclist' from Rosegrove and 'Long de Dong' the match seller. This selection, which includes many previously unpublished photographs, pays tribute to the way this fascinating town has been shaped over the years.

0-7524-1566-2

Chorley Then and Now
JACK SMITH

The changing face of Chorley is captured here with a fascinating selection of over eighty old photographs each paired with a modern view taken from the same vantage point. The old Lancashire market town reappears before our eyes with scenes of vanished streets and buildings, the railway station, the canal, fairs and the market. This book will appeal to all who enjoy nostalgic trips into the past and it will certainly be an eye-opener for anyone who thinks that 'not much changes in Chorley'!

0-7524-2278-2

If you are interested in purchasing other books published by Tempus, or in case you have difficulty finding any Tempus books in your local bookshop, you can also place orders directly through our website

www.tempus-publishing.com